Damaged Children
Healing Hearts to Love Again

TAREN WALTON

This book or parts thereof may not be reproduced in any form, stored in a retrieval system or transmitted in any form by any means - electronic, mechanical, photocopy, recording or otherwise - without prior written permission of the publisher, except as provided by United States of America copyright law.

Unless otherwise noted, all Scripture quotations are from the King James Version. Copyright © 1995, The Zondervan Corporation. Used by permission.

Scripture quotations marked AMP are from the Amplified Bible. Old Testament Copyright © 1962, 1964, 1965, 1987, by the Zondervan Corporation. The Amplified New Testament Copyright © 1954, 1958, 1987 by the Lockman Foundation. Used by permission.

Edited and Proofread by
Shantasha K. Love of Elite Graphixz Design & Publishing

Layout & Printed by
Shantasha Love of Elite Graphixz Design & Publishing

Copyright © 2018 by Elite Graphixz Design & Publishing
All Rights Reserved to Taren Walton

Library of Congress Cataloging-in-Publication International Standard Book Number: 978-1984126405

Printed in the United States of America
First Printing: January 2018

Published by Elite Graphixz Design & Publishing
3006 S. Jefferson Avenue – Saint Louis, MO 63118
info@egraphixz.com – 314.337.4143
Touching the World One Book at A Time!

DAMAGED CHILDREN
HEALING HEARTS TO LOVE AGAIN

TAREN WALTON

TABLE OF CONTENT

Chapter	Title	Page
	Forward	6
	Dedication	10
	Introduction	11
One	When Suffering Hurts	13
Two	A Daddyless Daughter	33
Three	My Miracles & Blessings	45
Four	Imitation of Life	61
Five	Matters of the Heart	74
Six	A Praying Wife & Mother	88
Seven	Salvation in the Eyes of Me	97
Eight	From Pain to Purpose	108

Damaged Children
Healing Hearts to Love Again

Taren Walton

FORWARD
Lady LeShae J. Tyson

Pain, particularly emotional pain, is a universal language. No matter your race, cultural background, ethnicity, age, or economic status; you have experienced pain. Emotional pain can be extremely difficult to overcome, in fact, some never recover. More difficult than overcoming the pain is telling your story to others. That is exactly what Taren has done with so much transparency and honesty, tell her story. Taren's story is raw and marbled with hardship, but I love that her story did not silence her.

The enemy uses the complexity and shame of our pain to silence us. Our mouths are closed, and we have wounds that are wide open. The Bible tells us that we overcome by the blood of the lamb and by the word of our testimony. Taren is living out the word of God by overcoming through her testimony.

Upon meeting Taren a few years ago, she began to share with me the intimate details of her life. I immediately admired her bravery to share with me, one person, and her journey through what sounded like bottomless pit. I have also been honored to watch parts of the transformation and growth in her life and the lives of her family members. Taren started with principle thing, prayer. Then she began sharing her testimony, her words, and her truth. Now, with this book, her words will reach thousands. Thousands who are in pain, thousands who are in depression, thousands who are discouraged, thousands who are crying out in despair, thousands who are suffering in silence, thousands asking God to send help.

This book is the relief many people have been praying for. God has allowed Taren to survive extreme adversity, navigating a life no child or young adult should have to endure. She has stood through the fire, corrected some wrongs, forgave, and has been forgiven to be the beacon of light someone else needs to fight through their suffering and torment. God has allowed her to be an overcomer to usher others, through her words, to a place of hope. God has allowed others to see, through Taren, that there is a win on the other side of what has you wounded.

My prayer is that as you read this book you will see that you don't just have to endure, but you can have and live a life of expectancy. You don't have to allow the anger to fester, but you can greet life with anticipation and rise to be greater. You don't have to what until the promise to rejoice, you can allow God to use this book to change your perspective while you're praying for transition and change.

I pray that Taren's words on these pages provoke you to go and tell someone. Tell someone through the tears, tell someone through anger, tell someone through what just may be just a whisper, release a heart that has been hiding behind bloodied scars.

I say to you, figuratively and literally, turn the page. Healing is on the horizon!

DEDICATION

I would like to dedicate this book to my Lord and savior, because of him I am who I am today I am so grateful that he loved me with his grace to save me when I couldn't save myself and for that I am forever grateful. I would like to thank my husband and children who loved me unconditionally through my mistakes, thanking God that he has touched our hearts to love each other through our process.

INTRODUCTION

This book is for people like me that have experienced adversities in their lives that have caused each and every one of us to feel unloved, depressed, suicidal, even attempted suicide, some of us have even looked for fulfillment in different ways that may have seemed good at first but it left us feeling disappointed and empty on the inside this pain have caused us to deal with pain of the past and matters of the heart.

Through my journey of pain and suffering and becoming damaged goods I am grateful to God for the revelation he has given me about his love it has truly changed my life and I am convinced that this book will change your life and the lives of your family and that he will heal the very depth of your soul.

-Taren Walton

CHAPTER ONE

WHEN SUFFERING HURTS

And God of all grace, who called you to his eternal glory in Christ, after you have suffered a little while, will himself restore you and make you strong, firm and steadfast. 1 Peter 5:10

WHEN SUFFERING HURTS

I was born to Mr. James and Mrs. Onita Brown. I am the second of seven children. I was born in St. Louis, Missouri. I am married to the wonderful Mr. Jeffrey Walton. We have a wonderful life and we have just celebrated twenty blissful years of marriage. We have seven beautiful children and sixteen healthy grandchildren, but it was at the tender age of ten that my life as a child was interrupted.

My mother had a live-in boyfriend who we thought loved us as his own, but he soon became abusive in more ways than one. He began to touch us in unwanted places and forced us to do the same to him on countless occasions. My mother worked overnight and didn't know what was going on. He would drop her off at work and we would be in fear when we heard the key enter the lock, despising his return. We would play sleep; but that did not work. Although the girls were forced to endure the molestation, the entire house experienced the mental, emotional, verbal and physical abuse. Even as a child, I can remember wondering why a mother would stay with a person that abuses her and her children.

Shortly afterward, she lost her job. As I reflect, I remember thinking – she is unemployed with seven children, nowhere to go and no one to turn to. I realized at that very moment – We were stuck! There were days when he made simple excuses just to beat all of us. He would use whatever was in reach at the time. He would even force us to fight with one another as if we were in a boxing ring, causing our rage to extend from the living room to the classroom and beyond. We became angry children, always mad at each other and others. This type of abuse went on for years.

The day had come when my sister and I had had enough. My mother was gone for the day and we had mustered up enough strength and a strong enough bond with one another to sneak out of the house and report the abuse. By the time my mother had returned home, the police had been called and he had already been removed from the house. Finally, things would be different – so we thought. The courts had reassured us that he would never return to the house and we were happy to get our childhood back. Little did we understand the effects that this would have on our mom? We watched her have a severe nervous breakdown, for several days we did not see our mother and did not know where she was. Later, we were informed that she was in the hospital and we were sent to be watched by our grandmother. I must admit that I felt a sense of relief. I knew that our suffering was over, but little did I know - My life was just beginning!

Because of the molestation, I became interested in boys at an early age. I started dating at fourteen and by the age of fifteen, I gave birth to my first child. No one knew the physical, verbal and emotional abuse that I had once again embraced. Being quiet was the norm for this family, and since I had already been through all of this before it was easy to cover up the abuse. I hid every bruise; and I would make sure to lock the door when I would take showers and baths. But even through the abuse, I felt loved. I didn't know any better, because it felt good – But it would also hurt! Several times I would break up with him and then feel sorry for him and take him back. As time went on the abuse began to get worse!

I remember it like it was yesterday. A simple argument, nothing serious. I was amazed at how angry he had gotten so quickly. Next thing I know, I was being dragged down at least fifteen steps by the roots of my hair – With my child on my hip! I could taste the blood in my mouth as my head hit every step and my back braced me for the next painful collision – but something gave me enough strength to hold on to my child. Once I landed in the stairwell, I hid my son between the bannister and the door and tried to protect him as he screamed for me – while looking in the eyes of his father. The love of my life was now punching me, and kicking me, saying things to me that no woman should ever hear – and no son should ever hear his father say to his mother. I could feel the bruises forming all over my body. After exhaustion, he finally pushed my already beaten and bruised body down the last flight of stairs. I tumbled all the way down the stairs – yet cradling my son in my bruised arms. Once I landed, he found enough strength to kick me one concluding time. As I laid there, all I could think was – Wow, I'm still alive? But I did not move – I could not move. My entire body tormented with pain – my arms, my legs, my back, my hair. I laid in the same spot. As I laid there, I began to ask myself, "Why everyone that loves me, hurt me?"

He did not even help me up, but he later retrieved his son. I unpeeled my body off the floor heartbroken and battered, but I knew I had to fight on for the sake of my son. But that night while I laid in my bed, I had the opportunity to soberly reflect on that night's occurrence. Knowing the magnitude of threat my son was in, gave me the strength that I needed to walk away. That very night I made up my mind that this was it for me. I refused to take any more.

The next day, I told him I was done. He did not take it well – I expected that! For the first time ever, I was no longer fearful. If I made it through the last beating, I would make it through this one. I told him that I was no longer scared and as I began to walk away he hit me – and I hit him back! It shocked him at first. But there was a new sense of independence that had come over me and I was determined to fight for my life – and for the life of my child. It was at this point, the boxing ring days with my siblings replayed in my head. With each blow I threw at him, I recalled each punch he threw at me at previous occasions. All the anger and aggression all came out at once – and he digressed! He simply stopped! I was ready to fight – but he stopped! And then he started to cry. What the hell? But I did not care about his tears. I did not care how much he said he loved me. I did not care how much he said he needed me. I walked away, and it was like a burden was lifted from my shoulders. I felt renewed, refreshed, restored – *revived*.

I slowly began to long for the love of my biological father. Why was he not around? If he was here, this would have never happened. Why didn't he want me? I felt rejected and unloved by the man that was supposed to love me and teach me the importance of loving myself. Now of course my mother loved me, but it was not the same. Therein lies the saying – I continued to look for love in all the wrong places. I continued to become promiscuous with other men – not as a remedy, but as an excuse.

At the age of seventeen, I had been raped by a class mate and was scared to tell anyone because *again* being quiet about things had become the norm. As I recalled the night, I couldn't help but wonder why did I deserve this life? Why must I continue to be misused and abused? I couldn't sleep that night because I was so hurt, and I felt so nasty. Even despite the various men I had given my body to, it was something different about being violated and it being taken against my will. I showered all night trying to wash away the filth. Regardless to the many times I showered, my mind kept rehearsing the rape repeatedly.

By twenty-one, I had given birth to all four of my children. In my early twenties, my children and I were still living with my mother. Things begin to fall apart. My mom and I were evicted from the house. It was then that I knew that my mom and I would have to separate. I did not want to leave my mom, but she was moving with her sister and my aunt did not have enough room for me and my children. I reached out to several family members and no one had the space for me and my kids

– except for one cousin. She agreed to allow us to stay with her, but despite the need, I declined because I did not want to raise my children in that environment and area that she lived in. In fact, I still had a couple of weeks at the house before I had to leave.

At this point I had learned to count my blessings. I was working on a decent job, we still had a roof over our heads, and food to eat – I would make this work for the time being. When I would leave for work, I instructed my kids to always keep the doors locked and to never go outside until I got home. Well, a neighbor noticed what was going on and she offered to keep an eye on the kids for me while I was at work – allowing them to go outside during the day and play – things were beginning to look up for me.

The time had come for us to move out of the house. My grandmother reached out to me and offered for my children to come and stay with her until I could get settled – but I could not stay! My grandmother never really accepted me. I never really understood why, but she would always mistreat me. Later in life, my mother explained to me why she did not like me. It's rather sad because her reasoning had absolutely nothing to do with me – but that was her reality at the moment. This proposition left me with one of the most difficult decisions of my life – leave my children. Although it was a difficult decision, it was an easy conclusion. Being as though I did not have a roof over my head, I knew that she would care for them, feed them, love them, and provide for them! For several nights, I would wait until she went to sleep and I would sneak into the house and spend the night with my children, but she found out one day and made me leave. I believe that a family member told her!

As I left my grandmother's house, leaving my children behind, I wondered where I would go. I went to my boyfriend's house, who is now my current husband, at the time he was still living with his parents. It started off as just spending a couple of nights over there. He told his parents what was going on and surprisingly they agreed to allow me and the kids to stay there with them. We were both employed, and we did not have babysitters so the decision was made to allow them to stay with my grandmother. It was not the greatest decision, but it was the best decision for the circumstance. I would pick them up on the weekends and take them back on Sundays. This was difficult for me as a mother, because to my family members, I looked to them as an unfit mother. They read my misfortune as me abandoning my children to go and live with another man and his family – this was so not the case! Therefore, being under the pressure of being talked about and ridiculed, I went and got my kids from my grandmother, but it added extra stress to my already stressful situation. Every morning now I would get up, get them ready and catch the bus to take them to school. I would get off the bus, cross the street, drop them off; only to have to cross the street, to wait on a bus going in the same direction to get to work. One day I was talking with the bus driver about this daily routine. He encouraged me and told me how strong of a young lady I was. I did not feel strong, in fact, I was ready to give up - I was tired! Then, surprisingly the next day he offered to wait for me to cross the street with my children and return and get back on his bus. I later realized, God's favor on my life concerning that situation – God was smiling on me even then.

We started looking for a place together. Although it was not very easy considering our income, we knew that the current living arrangements were temporary. I even signed up for Section 8 Housing. About 6 weeks later, I received a call from the Housing Authority that I was approved for a place in The Cochran Housing Apartments. Again, I kindly declined. I refused to raise three boys and a daughter in that atmosphere and environment. *I know what you're thinking*, how dare I turn down housing when I had nowhere to go? Well, I did! And I am glad I did. Needless to say, we continued to search, and we were approved for an apartment of my standards. And for the first time in a long time, things were getting better – but I was still depressed. I was happy on the outside, and still in a broken place on the inside.

Even though I was surrounded by all this love I felt that I had no one to talk too. I was lonely, empty – tired of faking happiness. I kept a lot of things from my mom, it wasn't until recently that she even learned of the rape. As we spoke about it, she said that she could recall that day. She knew that something was wrong, but she just could not put her finger on it. She even remembered that I cried all that day. I remember her asking me, but I knew that she had been through a lot and I did not feel that at the time that she was healthy enough to deal with my issues – or so I thought.

At the age of 35, my mom received Christ. Slowly, but surely as she learned, she began to teach us to pray. I remember at an early age accepting the Lord as my personal savior and the confession that I was saved, but I still did not serve God according to the scriptures. But even when I would try to hang out with my family and friends, I always felt rejected. They did things that I did not do – I did not smoke or drink – and even when I tried to fit in, I still felt rejected. I remember several times going to the clubs and parties with my friends and pretending to have fun, but I would be so bored and miserable – but more so depressed. In a crowed club, I felt so alone and no one to talk to – even my boyfriend. He was broken himself, he could not help me. We were going through tough times and although he told me that he loved me and did everything to show me - I still felt unloved and completely alone.

Suicidal thoughts began to invade my mind. I thought then I wouldn't have to worry about the pain anymore. So, I did it... I took a *whole* bottle of pills. My boyfriend found me laying on the bed and rushed me to the hospital. Dazed but coherent, I remember the doctors coming into the room and telling me to drink the substance in this small white cup. He said that if I did not drink the cup, they would have to pump my stomach and that it would be rather painful. Well I was tired of pain, so I drunk the cup. As I laid there in the bed rehearsing what I had done, I conversed with myself for the moment – Did I really want to die, or had I done this just for attention? I realized that the answer was yes to both questions. I was tired.

The counselor came in. She talked to me. She listened to me – That was all I needed, someone to listen. She listened for hours, I told her everything. Once I released it all, to my amazement she promised not to admit me to the psych ward nor would she place this incident on my permanent file. She realized that I was just reaching out for help. I was not a threat to anyone – including myself. I understood that God had a plan for my life and that he was setting up my destiny and my purpose. All the pain and suffering that I have endured were for this testimony. All the prayers that my mother prayed for me were not in vain. And although I do not have a full understanding of everything that I endured and all that I suffered, I take comfort in knowing that I am alive to tell the story of what to do ...*When Suffering Hurts.*

Damaged Children
Healing Hearts to Love Again

Taren Walton

CHAPTER TWO

A DADDYLESS DAUGHTER

A father to the fatherless a defender of widows, is God in his holy dwelling God sets the lonely in families he leads forth the prisoners with singing but the rebellious live in a sun scorched land. Psalms 68: 5-6

A DADDYLESS DAUGHTER

I remember as a child longing for the love of my father whom I didn't get to see often. I know that my mother and father were once married, but I don't remember living in the house with my father. I remember going to spend the weekends with him at my grandmother's house. I would enjoy our visits so much and often I couldn't wait to go back to his house. Suddenly, the visits stopped, and I did not see my father for a long time. Several times he would come to see us, but he was not allowed to. I don't know why – and I never asked, but I would lay in my bed and cry because I wanted to spend time with him. I would see friends with their fathers living in their homes and it would remind me that my father was not at home. As I became an adult I realized you can be in the home and still be an absent parent. There are fathers that spend little to no time with their children and don't teach them anything. As I grew up I would see my father in passing. I remember once seeing my dad afar off one day while I was out with my friends, I was so ashamed and embarrassed at how drunk he was that I did not even acknowledge him.

I will never forget the day that I found out that my dad and his girlfriend moved across the street from our home. I was so excited that he was so close, and I will finally get to spend some much-needed time with my father. By this time, I had already had my first child and I could not wait for him to meet his grandson. My dad was so proud, and they immediately built a bond that was second to none. My dad would ask if my son could spend the night my mother disagreed, but I made sure to take my son by to visit him every day. It was important for my son to have something that I wanted. For so many years, I had longed for this exact thing. I was so happy. Just to have him there, near me, touchable, and to talk to.

One day, I went to his house after school and he had moved! No warning, no goodbye – He was gone! He had not been there long, maybe three months, but those were the best three months of my short life. Through my tears and desperation that day I made a vow that I would find my dad again. While out with my cousin I just happened to see him on the street. I was happy again. His presence brought me joy and contentment. He gave me his new address and it turned out he was now just around the corner from my house. My joy increased even more. I was thrilled with the fact that my brother James, my son and I could start back visiting him. We visited every day for months. My mom had one rule – We had to stop by the house first before going to see our dad and to return by curfew. I couldn't wait to get out of school every day, I just wanted to be around my dad all the time.

He loved the oldies and that was our pastime. He would play old school songs like the Temptations and I would sit on his lap and sing along with him. He would tell me that he loved me, this was all I had been waiting for - to hear those three words, and he would tell us that every time it was time for us to go home. After a while my sister and other brother would go over and visit. I remember it would make me so happy when my friends would ask me what I was doing for the weekend, and I could finally respond – Going to my dad's house with the biggest smile on my face!

Although I was excited to be with him, I felt that my dad was just as happy to be with me. He was equally as happy to spend time with his grandson, but little did he know I was pregnant with my second child. His girlfriend told him that I was pregnant, but when he asked me I denied it, because I did not want him to be disappointed in me. To this day I regret that I did not tell him. I covered my lie, every time I would visit I would try to hold my stomach in, or I wore big clothes. In my mind, I concluded that I would reveal my secret when I go into labor – maybe then he would not be upset with me. Instead he would be happy about the birth of his second grandchild.

One day, I left as normal to go home to prepare for school. He was laying on the couch complaining of a stomachache. He kissed my son and I kissed him and brushed his hair – he had the prettiest cold black wavy hair! He would let me play in his hair all the time. I would give him a long braid or brush it up in a long ponytail. He loved for me to comb his hair just as much as I enjoyed combing his hair. Even on the way to school, I was excited about seeing my father later that day. As I walked through the hall to change classes, my cousin ran up to me, said sorry for your loss and that she didn't think I would be at school today. I asked her what she was referring to and she said about your dad. She was the one that gave me the most devastating news – My dad passed away last night! I thought maybe she was confused because I was just with my dad last night. I knew he was not feeling well but I didn't think that it was that serious. What really bothered me was I shared a class with my dad's girlfriend's daughter and she didn't say anything to me.

My name was called over the intercom – immediately I knew it was true. My aunt and mother were waiting for us in the principal office to take us home. Anger over took me, and I remember wanting to beat up his step daughter for not telling me that my dad had passed while we were in class. Thirty-six years old and we were preparing for his funeral. I was so devastated. But my mom allowed us to play a part in planning the funeral. My mom and dad were still married; so my uncle paid for the funeral, which left his girlfriend without any say in the arrangements. She wanted to cut his hair; but we were totally against that. We cried to my mom and begged her not to cut his hair; she looked at the funeral director and told them to do what we wanted. We were so proud! We felt that we had honored my dad's wishes and it felt good to have a say over my dad for the first time in my life.

As I prepared to get dressed, I thought about the moments that we had spent, and I smiled through my tears. Dressing my son, I thought about the baby in my stomach - that he will never see, and the remorse grew stronger. Viewing him in the casket, I remember that I smiled and cried at the same time, because a part of me knew that I would miss him dearly, but I smiled in admiration because God had granted me the chance to spend time with my dad. I got the chance to hear him tell me that he loved me. I got the chance to sit in his lap and play in his hair.

The burial site was very difficult for me. This was my first funeral and I just wanted to see his face one more time and I did not know that they could not open the casket. I begged, and I cried. I essentially lost it! All I wanted was to see his face one more time, but they would not allow it! Days had passed by and all I could do was think of him. His smile, his voice, his smell...I prayed for him to come back. I felt lonely all over again – *unloved*. I gave birth to my second child. I stared at him for a very long time and told myself that my dad would have loved to see him. I still think of the time that I spent with my dad. Even now it makes me smile to know that I was given a year to get to know my dad – although it felt like a lifetime.

As I reflect on the several encounters I endured, I often wonder, would I have gone through these things if he were there? Would I have embraced so much suffering? Although these thought haunt me, I know that I will never know the answers to any of them. I resolve my displeasure with the fact that he left a smile on my face, this is a part of me that I will always cherish for the rest of my life. I will continue to speak with other young ladies about being without their fathers.

This has become my passion; to keep them from making the same mistakes that I made - looking for love in all the wrong places. I thank God for my testimony, He is the only one that can feel the void. I will always love and cherish my father. Thank you for your love and support, James Percy Brown.

Signed, *A Daddyless Daughter*

DAMAGED CHILDREN
HEALING HEARTS TO LOVE AGAIN

TAREN WALTON

CHAPTER THREE

MY MIRACLES AND BLESSINGS

Children are a heritage from the Lord, offspring a reward from him. Psalms 127:3

MY MIRACLES AND BLESSINGS

I am the proud and esteemed mother of four beautiful children. There is a miracle and blessing in each one of them. I again reflect on the moment that I found out that I was pregnant with my first child. I was only fifteen years old. Every month I would leave school and sneak to the Parent Planhood not far from my house. I wanted to tell someone, but I just could not take the chance of anyone telling my mom. So I told no one. It literally ate me up inside, and it caused me to be sad and secluded most of the time. I refrained from eating a lot because I did not want to get big. It was definitely my intentions to hide this pregnancy until the birth of my baby.

One day I woke up for school and I was very sick. Not nausea, but very weak and dizzy-like. I assume that I passed out, because I awoke to my mom calling my name. She glanced down at my shirt and I watched in horror as her eyes latched to my belly in disbelief. She stared at the little pudge in my stomach and she looked me directly in my eyes. She asked me what was wrong. I shrugged that I did not know. She stared in disbelief at my stomach again and asked me if I was I pregnant?

I did not know exactly how to answer. I was already vulnerable lying on the floor. How would she react? What will she do? Should I continue my plan, or was this the ending to my deception? In a low toned voice, I digressed to the truth. A calm overtook me – I finally shared my secret. The silence was deafening. The disappointment on her face was abysmal. With tears in her eyes she helped me up and walked me to her bedroom. She sat with me on her bed and expressed her disappointment. She explained to me that I was too young to have a baby and that she did not want me to destroy my life. She confessed that I had a bright future ahead of me and that she suggested that I have an abortion. I told her that I wanted to keep my baby, she responded that she would make an appointment tomorrow morning at the clinic.

Her calmness frightened me. As I prepared for the appointment, I was not afraid. We waited in the waiting room – We exchanged no words. The counselor called my name, but told my mom that I had to come into the room alone. While in the examination room, we talked candidly. She asked me if this was something that I wanted to do, and I told her that I did not. She then asked me why was I there, and I shared with her that my mom was making me have the procedure. She looked at the chart and said that she was going to have the doctor come in and do an exam. I smiled, I knew exactly what that meant.

After the exam, my mom was invited in the room and the doctor explained to my mom that I could not get the abortion because I was due in two weeks. I knew that I was much further along than my mom thought - I did not know I was nine months, but I knew I was too far long to get an abortion. Things immediately took a swift turn. My mom looked at me and told me that everything would be OK. I guess when she realized that this was actually going to happen, she began to accept that this would be her first grandchild. I remember her coming home with clothes and boxes. She bought me everything that she thought that I and the baby needed. She enrolled me in an alternative school for expectant mothers because back then we could not go to regular school. This was a great solution for me, it made me comfortable and I was no longer ashamed – for two full weeks I was actually able to enjoy my pregnancy.

Every week we would go to bible study at the neighbor's house. She led my mom to Christ and taught her to be a woman of prayer. One day at bible study, our neighbor began to prophecy to me – I did not know anything about prophecy – but she confirmed it was real when she told me that I was having a boy. She told me that God said that my baby boy was in the palm of his hand and that he would hold him and wrap him in his arms. And that no harm would come near his dwelling until the day he dies. I did not understand those words then, but I definitely understand those words today.

Needless to say, I gave birth to a healthy baby boy. Shortly after his birth, my mom and her friends prayed over his life and gave him back to God. A year and a half later and I discovered – I'm pregnant again! Seventeen years old and living with another secret. My dad was in my life, so now I had the task of hiding it from both parents. But this pregnancy was different from the last one. I was sick during my first trimester and I was unable to hold down any food. I remember calling the father and telling him that I was pregnant. I thought that he would be happy – he was not. In fact, he told me to abort the baby or he would leave me. Again, this was not an option. I was devastated, but I wanted to keep my baby, with or without him.

I began crumbling under the pressure of hiding this secret, a single mother already taking care of one son, constantly feeling sick, trying to handle the current pregnancy alone – and then the death of my father. This was too much for a teenager to handle. I fell into a state of depression and could no longer hide the secret from my mom. She was upset, but sympathetic with everything that life was throwing at me. She re-enrolled me back into the alternative school, and surprisingly, I was reacquainted with girls that attended with me the first time I was there. Once I hit my second trimester, the pregnancy was a lot easier. There were no complications or concerns - Accept during labor, the doctor almost dropped my son on the floor. This really frightened me. I could only imagine what the outcome would have been if it would have happened. Second child, seventeen years old – but things were just getting started.

Couple of year later, and Yes, you guessed it! I was pregnant again. By this time, I was mentally strained and did not want anything to do with having another child. I knew that I could not afford to have any abortion, so I devised a plan to kill the baby myself. I regret even speaking these words now – but this was my reality at the time. I knew that I could not bring this heartbreak to my mom again. I would turn flips and do cartwheels; I would purposely fall on my stomach – any activity I could conjure up to make the baby's umbilical cord wrap around its neck. I tried this for months, but nothing was successful. My mom was out of town, but returned unexpectedly; so unaware and off guard, I was sleep in the room and one of my siblings told her that I was pregnant. She came in the room and saw me and she went into a screaming fit! She said things to me that I have never heard her say, I cried for weeks. I was hurt, discouraged – broken. Eventually, things began to look up and my mom began to come around and except the pregnancy.

After two boys, I asked God for a girl; and sure, enough the ultrasound revealed that she was a girl! The excitement grew throughout the family. I imagined how I would dress her and comb her hair and fix her room. While playing with my brother I experienced the worst pain ever in my side. I thought it was nothing, but then it hit me again – I knew it as time. I remember getting to the hospital and being rolled down a long hall – I thought that it would never end. I felt the urged to push, but I was told not to push. She was coming so fast and I could not control it. I remember gritting my teeth and holding my breath trying not to push, but with each contraction it became harder and harder not to push. She was coming, and before I could even get my clothes off she was crowning. When she arrived - silence!

I waited to hear for the sound of my baby's cry. I looked in despair. I asked the nurse why my baby was not crying. She told me everything was going to be okay. I looked over and saw my baby blue in color, limp with no sound. The doctor spanked her several times – no cry. I asked another nurse what was going on. She promised to be straight with me. She told that my baby was not breathing and that she may not make it. I asked her to call for my mother so that she could pray for her. Tears begin to roll down my face. The memories of the several times that I tried to kill my baby rushed through my head. But things had changed. I loved my baby now and I wanted her to live. I prayed for God to spare my child's life. I heard the doctor call a code blue. People were running in with crash carts and screaming all kinds of medical terminology. I began to pray for forgiveness. I told God that I was sorry for trying to kill her and I begged him to please let her live. At that exact moment she started to cry! The doctor cancelled the code and the room calmed down. I wanted to hold her, but they said that they had to take her and check her out first. I was so ashamed, nobody knew what I had done to try and kill her – But God still gave me my miracle.

A few years later, I found myself pregnant again. For months I did not know that I was pregnant because I continued to have my regular menstrual cycles. I made a doctor's appointment because I did not feel well. I remember him asking me how many children I had. I thought that as a strange question. I told him that I had three. He said, "Well, prepare for four!" I was in pure disbelief! I argued that I was on birth control and that this was impossible.

About a month later, I scheduled another appointment because I was experiencing severe stomach pain. I was told that I had a tumor and that I needed to terminate or abort the pregnancy. At this point I was so tired of hearing the word abortion, but with no resolve I decided again that this was not an option for me. I was advised by my doctor that if I did not abort the pregnancy, my child could die, or I could die – or both. I told him that I would trust God and take that risk.

As the pregnancy progressed, so did the complications. There were times I would break out in hives so bad, that I could not sleep from the pain. The tumors became so unbearable at times; it became an impossible task to walk. I was told that my weight would double in size because of the tumor, and that is exactly what happened. One night, our house caught on fire and burned completely to the ground. We all had to move in my grandmother, which was stressful for me because I knew that my grandmother did not like me, and she would constantly mistreat me. I became depressed through the endurance of constant verbal abused from my grandmother which cause me to threaten a miscarriage. The doctor told my mom that something has me very stressed and that he needed to place me on bed rest for the remainder of the pregnancy or the baby would not make it. My mom knew that my grandmother was causing my stress and, so she would rent motel rooms for me to get rest and a peace of mind.

During, my last trimester I had a car accident and hit a pole which caused me to go into labor. The early conversations with my doctor rushed my mind as I went into labor causing a sense of fear to come upon me. But I had to put my trust in God and believe that he would bring me and my child through this labor. As the labor progress, I was told that my baby was breach, and regardless to all the doctor's effort she decided to do a C-Section. At the last minute, he turned but there was still a problem to get him out. The doctor noticed that my son was at risk of aspirating meconium. This caused an urgent need to get him out, so she used forceps to remove him which caused him to be swollen from all the drama of the birth and placed on observation. I was so exhausted I couldn't even hold him, but I was glad we both made it!

Through it all, I am blessed to have four of the greatest children. I will always be grateful to the gifts that God gave me, they will always be - My Miracles and Blessings!

Damaged Children
Healing Hearts to Love Again

Taren Walton

CHAPTER FOUR

IMITATION OF LIFE

Therefore, be imitators of GOD, as beloved children. Ephesians 5:1

Imitation of Life

I remember as a child wanted to be just like my mother. Some of her attributes were good and some were bad – but she was *my* mother. As a child, I would watch her put on make-up and prepare to go out with her friends. I would tell her how cute she'd look, and I remember always thinking I wanted to be just like her when I grow up. As I watched my mother there were very low days; but there were some high days too; especially when she finally became free from her abuser. After her nervous breakdown, she was fortunate enough to find another job – she had seven children to take care of now all along because neither of our fathers were present in our lives. This proved to be a difficult task even with her job. She worked multiple shifts a day just to provide, which caused her to be so tired all the time. Things began to take a turn for the worst and it became apparent that she was not making enough money to care for all her children. I remember time when the lights and the heat were off. I still recall day that we were hungry and did not know when to expect the next decent meal.

Although we were too young and could not work, we really wanted to help mom because we knew that she was doing all that she could to take care of us – Not just because we were her children, but she made it very clear that she loved us. There were times that she would align us up one by one and tell each of us individually how much she loved us. She would give us these long and tight hugs – there are no doubt that we were loved. And although we did not have the finer things in life, she was great at teaching us about life and showing love and affection to one another. She struggled many days to care for us, but she never gave up on us.

Now, as much as she loved us – she also disciplined us. And sometime the whippings were so bad, we may have felt at the moment unloved and abused. But I have learned in my adulthood that children never take responsibility for their disobedience and rebellion and are rather quick to blame a parent for being abusive versus being a disciplinarian. And although I felt that several time my mother went overboard on more than a few of my whippings – and she admits that she made several mistakes – I can take in account that I deserved more than few of those whippings. She also had a way with words. I believe unknowingly and due to the stress of trying to provide for her family, she later became very verbally abusive. Things that she would say out of frustration would make us cry and would hurt our feelings, especially coming from such a loving woman.

Now in my opinion, some of my other siblings were more rebellious than me. But because of her disciplinary strategy, we would all get a whipping. This caused a lot of anger and resentment to one another. There were times that I wanted to run away from home – crossed my mind thousands of times - But I had nowhere to go. Now in my mom defense, we were no angels. Some would steal, others were boosting clothes, we were all sexually active at an early age and all she knew to do was beat it out of us. Some of us have forgiven her for the abuse – some have not.

I for one have forgiven my mother for everything. She was in denial of the abuse for several years until one day we sat down together and talked about the pain that I was feeling. I had tried several times before, but she was not ready. But in her own timing the conversation was welcomed and much needed – for both parties. We both cried, we laughed, it took some time, but we are both free of the pain from the past.

It is unsettling that my mom and other siblings are not close – which causes the extended families not to be close. In most family the grandmother would hold the family together, but unfortunately we have no one to hold us together. There is still a lot of animosity and resentment between siblings, but there proves to be no measure of desire to bridge the gap.

While we were still home my mother did start dating again. We liked him because we did not have to worry about money anymore because he owned his own business and he took great care of our mother. She was happy again – smiling, laughing, calmer. We could tell that she was in love with him, and we were happy because she was happy. Shortly, things took a bad turn. My mother found out that he was cheating, and as most women, she retaliated by fighting and tearing up stuff. She was so angry, but mostly hurt! We were back at the drawing board once again struggling to make ends meet.

Through her brokenness a neighbor was able to witness to my mother and tell her about the love of God. We started attending bible study and learning more about God's word.

This changed her life for the better. I saw a new found revelation and happiness that I had never saw in my mom's eyes before. I saw her reading the bible and praying every day. She started taking us to bible study and teaching us to pray and to foster a relationship with

God.

Now things had changed, although we were back in the place of struggle, mom positioned herself in a place of trusting God. Because of her new zeal for Christ, nobody could tell her that God wasn't going to provide for her family. I remember being saved at an early age because I did everything I thought my mother wanted me to do. I went to church with her all the time. I did everything she did because I wanted to be just like my mother. I'm talking about imitation because we tend to imitate others in both negative and positive ways. I became an imitator of doing what I thought my mother wanted me to do. Most of us imitate other people because we need to be motivated to be something that we are not or we lack inspiration due to fear. I thought if I didn't do it her way she would be angry at me.

I remember her ministering to people on the street and I would be right there with her walking along side of her. She became the mother of the neighborhood. People would walk up to her while sitting on her porch and talk with her all day. In my eyes and I am sure in hers as well, she was doing the work of the Lord. My mother was a praying woman she instilled the importance of prayer. My mother developed this learn behavior from her mother. We have to be careful with imitating the lives of others because it can become a pattern that will carry on into the lives of our children. I was guilty of imitating the way I was raised and disciplined. It took some time to realize that it was a learned behavior and that I imitated what I saw and what I heard - and what I had been through. I destroyed my children along the way. I tried to raise them the way I was raised, but I forgot how it made me feel unloved, and the anger that I had built on the inside of me.

It's easy to pick up someone else's habits, especially those that you're close to you. We can damaged our children for life if were not careful. This will lead to generational curses. Think back to when your child was two years old; that's when they begin to say what you said and do what you did. Therefore, we must be very careful with our babies. We must start somewhere. Negative learned behavior cannot continue like this. Our children are crying out for love. They are dealing with pain of the past. Not only do our children need prayer, but most of them also need professional help as well. But we as parents must get ourselves together because we've got work to do. We can't help them until we help ourselves.

I use to wonder what my kids will hold against me when they are older because of the mistakes that I have made. I am now dealing with issues with my adult children and it's not easy. I know that it's a long journey but I am trusting God to heal all of us it hurts sometimes I now know how my mother felt when her children were dealing with pain of the past and she didn't know what to do, but to give it to God. She can't force any of her children to forgive her. She has prayed and trust that God will soften the hearts of her children that are still hurting and to allow them to forgive her for her mistakes. But to achieve this milestone, she had to forgive herself. So, I imitated my mom again today and I for forgive myself for my errors in raising my children; while writing a meager version of her...Imitation of Life.

Damaged Children
Healing Hearts to Love Again

Taren Walton

CHAPTER FIVE

MATTERS OF THE HEART

He heals the broken hearted and binds up their wounds. Psalms 147:

Matters of the Heart

I have four children; three sons and one daughter. They are the love of my life. When my children were born, I told myself that I would be the best mother in the world. I promised to spin time with them and take them to fun places. They were so adorable. I didn't want them to grow up but as they did, they all assumed their own identity. At times they were so funny, and they would make me laugh. I would love to hug and kiss on them but as they all begin to enter kindergarten; one by one it became clear that they were all growing up. There was a part of me that didn't want to let them go.

Once they got older, then started the sibling rivalry. My daughter was the only girl and she refused to back down from her brothers. She was very outspoken and often said what she felt, and she didn't care if you accepted it or not. My oldest son was different from all my children. He was humble, and all wanted to be the peacemaker. It took a lot to get him angry. He would ignore the others. He was very respectful when I would talk to him. When he did get in trouble, he never said anything in defense. He would just let me talk and he would immediately apologize afterwards. All my children were very smart in school, but my oldest son we considered a genius.

My second son was a little different. He always had to debate what was said. He always felt that he had to get his thoughts across and that he was never understood. He would always say, "Kids have opinions too!" it was not until later that I realized that he was right.

My baby boy was a little different he didn't have much

to say until he became a teenager and then he begin to become very opinionated. He would speak loudly as if that would help get his point across. I would try to figure out why he yelled so much. But all he cared about was being right and being heard. I couldn't deal with the loud tone, so I would walk away, or I would tell him to call me and speak with me later when his tone comes down.

We as parents never know or could even imagine the inner strugglers that our children go through. One thing I know and have learned that the issues of life will show up and it will show up in areas you may have never imagined. I will never proclaim to be the perfect parent because God knows I made a million mistakes along the way. I have seen my children walk around with pain of the past, but I would ignore it because my mistakes were too embarrassing to address the effects. So, I would walk in denial regarding that things that they would say. I did this for a long time, but the time for accountability had finally come in 2016. I had to deal with an issue that I had been avoiding for a very long time.

One of my children had been carrying the burden of pain of the past for a long time. When my son wanted to talk it would come out in verbal anger with yelling and telling me the issues that he was experiencing, although I did not want to hear the truth. We all know that the truth hurts. I would hang the phone up or I would use an excuse to tell him he's being disrespectful, and I would hang the phone up. But that was my way of not having to deal with the truth.

One day I heard the Holy Spirit speak and tell me that it was time to listen to his heart and not his mouth. That was the hardest thing for me to do, because every word that came out of his mouth cut me so deep. He didn't know the tears that was flowing down my face as I listened to every word. I told God that my son not only needed prayer but that he also needed professional help. I made the decision to seek counseling for my son, but little did I know that God had a plan for me as well. I also needed the healing of the past because now I had realized that we both are dealing with matters of the heart.

I made an appointment for all my children and myself, but no one accepted the appointment but this child. He also knew that he needed professional assistance. I was fearful of what was going to be said at the meeting. Before we arrived, I tried to think of what my child could be hurting from and what he would say in the meeting. I realized that just because he was my child that didn't mean that I knew what he was going through and dealing with personally.

As the time approached for our first visit it became even more concerning for me. I begin to fast and pray daily. I remember telling God no matter how much the words would hurt me, I was determined to endure it because I needed my son to be free. I remember like it was yesterday I picked him up and as we were on our way we both were quiet because surely, we didn't know how the outcome would be. We both walk slowly down the hallway. I asked him if he was ready, he stated that he was. As we entered in the office we both were asked to sit down on the couch it reminded me of a T.V. Show. I remember her telling me that out of the 20 years of dealing with patients, she had never had a mother to come in with an adult child and that she wanted to shake my hand. That's when I knew it was God because he does the impossible.

She already knew why we there because she had been given an update on our situation She allowed my son to speak first and as he begin to speak tears begin to fall from his face. I begin to cry from the words that was being said. I had nowhere to run and no more excuses to give. It was time for me to show accountability. As I listened I became shocked. I slowly began to realize that I was visiting with a thirty-four-year-old adult that had a fourteen year old little boy on the inside that needed to be free from pain of the past. When I was asked how I felt about what he was saying, I told her that I take full responsibility and accountability for what he had endured. I begin to apologize and as I apologized my child cried even harder. It hurt me to see him in so much pain and to realize that we were both hurting on the inside. I had walked in denial for so long, but it felt good to be free from the lies and deceit. I knew God was with the both of us because we were able to cry and smile at the same time. It became easier as we continued with our appointments. We had finally gotten a breakthrough and we were both free from what was hidden all this time.

But this was far from over. I remember waking up one morning and preparing to pray. I clearly saw another one of my children as a child. God begin to take me down memory lane. What I began to see was ugly and very disturbing. I began to weep like a baby. I asked God why he was allowing me to see the hurt that my children had suffered – why had he waited so late. I saw the hurt, the confusion, the pain and the helplessness. I begin to pray and fast because I knew that this was not going to be an easy road to travel. I knew that God was going to continue what he started with my children – to heal my children and give them complete wholeness. I begin to prepare myself; knowing that God had already prepared me with the first child. I begin to talk with each of my children separately; to repent to God, then I told each of my children that I was sorry and that I would take accountability for their hurting hearts.

I stayed constantly in the face of God because I knew that this was too big for me and I wasn't going to move until he open that door completely. I recall talking to my daughter asking her was it something that I did that caused her to hurt. Being that she was my only daughter, we were very close, and I knew that she would tell me the whole truth. Now that I had finally had the courage to ask questions, I felt relieved when she told me that she wasn't hurting from anything, and perhaps since she was the only girl she felt that things may have been different for her. She felt protected more from me and my husband as a little girl and even into her adult life. She did however enlighten me on some of the mistakes that she felt that I made with the boys and how she felt that they may have been suffering and caring some emotional scars because of some of the mistakes that I made. I knew that she would be honest with me and I knew that she would not be judgmental – because she wanted total healing for the entire family – just as myself.

One thing that I have learned through this process is that when our children are hurting, it will reflect in some form or fashion throughout their life. The matter of life will present itself; either through pain, their behavior in school, drugs or alcohol, or looking for love in all the wrong places. As parents we are always quick to reference that our children are bad, and they are running with the wrong crowd, but in reality they are actually running from the pain in the home? When our children are broken, they either date or will marry another broken person, and it becomes a kindle of fire. We enter into relationships with men and women that's not a positive influence or even a great example for our children. We operate in the flesh to please our own desires. We ignore the red flags. We make it all about us and not about our children. When we look back over our life, we realize we should have did a better job at choosing the people that surrounded our children.

Matthew 17:21 teaches us that some things only going to come through fasting and praying. I know that it was nobody but God that opened the door to healing for both me and my children. I believe that it was only because of my obedience to fast and to pray that these doors were open. The hardest words to hear is from your child telling you that they thought you hated them because of the treatment that they had experienced as a child. Now I and all of my children are at a place of love, respect and adoration. We can smile and be honest with each other.

Learned behavior will damage your children, but God is a rewarder to them that diligently seek him. I've learned that my children are a promise; disguised as a problem and that all that they have been through - It was only for the glory of God. We can't allow our own children to be tore up, destroyed and damaged, but our only mission is to save a dying World. Yes, He does want us to be effective for His Kingdom, but we have to remember that ministry starts at home. I know the plans He have for us are of good and not of evil – and His plans are easily attainable because it's just a - *Matter of the Heart!*

DAMAGED CHILDREN
HEALING HEARTS TO LOVE AGAIN

TAREN WALTON

CHAPTER SIX

A PRAYING WIFE & MOTHER

Is any one of you in trouble He should pray? Is anyone happy let him sing songs of praises? James 5:13

A PRAYING WIFE & MOTHER

With all that has happened in our lives there was a time I thought that I was at a place of no return. But as I look back over my life and the life of my family, my soul cries out Hallelujah! There were times that I didn't know what to do with myself.

In chapter four, I talked about an Imitation of Life. One thing that I imitated from my mother was her prayer life. She as a praying mother. I would see her pray constantly over the lives of her children – especially her sons. I saw god answer her prayers and I would wonder how she could pray for hours at a time. Now that I have my own relationship with God, I understand that when you began to give him glory and look back at all that he had brought you through and the many blessings he has given, you just want to be in his presence and never let go.

I love the lord with all my heart - I am not perfect even in being in Christ. I have made plenty of mistakes. I have even played with God, having one foot in the world and one foot out of the world. I had become bored being in Christ and I began to focus on what appeared to be my friends enjoying life and I was letting it simply pass me by. Sin looks good to us when were not truly planted and rooted in the word of God.

While walking in disobedience one can become attracted to sin. We foster the mindset of thinking that we are having fun, when actually we are just craving for the things of the world. I have learned that cravings for the things of the world never goes away because once you obtain that one thing you begin to crave for something different. Cravings only fill a void just for a moment.

Even when I committed adultery, I thought that would fill the void in my life, but I still was unhappy because I knew that I was now in sin. And surprisingly, even in being in the arms of another man, I still felt lonely and all alone. Neither he nor my husband could fill the void that I had. But I learned from my mother even if you begin to stray away from Christ, don't stop praying and continue sitting under the word of God. So even in my sinful state, I stayed true to my prayer regimen and I continued to go to church. Every time I would hear the word of God, I would get so convicted. I would cry out at the altar knowing that I needed God to help me get out of the mess I was in. I knew that according to the word, I was living a life of sin. I even knew that things would soon fall apart, and that time would come for me to reap the sin that I had sewn. I remember the exact moment that things started falling apart in my household. I got a call that my brother had had a car accident and passed away. This was so devastating to me because we were so close. My heart was broken into so many pieces. I wonder was God trying to get my attention or was this the strength that I prayed for to get out of my mess. Either way I continued in sin.

Finally, I did become tired of the lifestyle that I was living and began to diligently seek God for strength to truly walk away. But I quickly learned again to be careful about what we ask for because we never know what situation God will allow us to go through to give us the strength that we need to come back to our first love in Him.

I promised God that regardless to what I would go

through in life, I would always be a witness to a woman in need. Well even through this situation, I met a woman at a new job that I started. Even in my brokenness I would minister life changing declarations to her. I would later go home and cry out to God like a little child and return to work the next day like I had everything together. No one knew the pain and the mental turmoil I was living. And right before my eyes God was doing miracles in their lives and he would set them free. I remain despondent wondering when my time would come for healing and restoration.

But I continued to pray and attend worship services. Then I got the news that my son was shot at – but got away with his life! Another son was arrested for a robbery that he did not commit. Then my daughter was in a car accident that looked worse than it was by the damage to the car. Then to top it all off, addiction hit my front door – and I found out that my husband was having an affair as well. I had finally saw the writing on the wall. I remember crying out to God with a sincere heart of repentance. Truly everything that I was enduring at one time gave me the strength that I needed to walk away from sin. I realized that we had open a door for the enemy to enter into our home and that we were now open to all kinds of spirits.

And often we wonder why our children, home and our marriages are torn apart. Most times it's because we have no covering and any covering that was there has been removed due to a sinful life. Everything that my mother had taught me about prayer had come back to me. Not only was she a praying woman she would always do praise and worship after her prayer time. And just as I imitated my mother before, I knew that my deliverance was in my praise and worship to Him. I knew that the victory had already been won, I just needed to get back into my rightful place in him. I went back to studying the word of God and I begin to fight with his word applied to my life.

I knew that his promises to me were still yes and amen and that every promise that he had spoken to me would still come to pass. I begin to remind him of that promise, and I would tell the devil that I'm going to come out of this with the help of God. After work I would come straight home go straight into my room and pray for hours and then do praise and worship. I begin to see God move in ways I had never seen before in the lives of my family. I understand so clearly now that if it had not been for the grace of God I don't know where I would be or where my family would be without the - *Life of a Praying Wife & Mother.*

Damaged Children
Healing Hearts to Love Again

Taren Walton

CHAPTER SEVEN

SALVATION IN THE EYES OF ME

Jesus looked at them and said, with man this is impossible but with God all things are possible. Matthew 19:26

SALVATION IN THE EYES OF ME

I receive Christ at an early age. As I mentioned in one of the early chapters, I only did this because it was what my mother wanted, and the plan was to always keep her happy. And although I did it for my mother, I did not realize that I was activating the destiny that God had ordained for me. I recall thinking the first few months that this would be easy. All I had to do was go to church on Sundays, hear the preacher preach, say my prayers at night – and I would go to heaven. But no one ever told me that this lifestyle would be so hard – and boring! No one disclosed the pain and the suffering that I would endure. Didn't God feel like I had suffered enough? I guess not. Yet I believed that serving the Lord would pay off awhile.

As the years went by, I began to feel that I was missing out on life. The ritual of church had become boring. So, as I mentioned earlier, I began to do all the things that I thought that I was big and bad enough to do – because I was grown! But I quickly had a reality check, realizing that sin only felt good for a moment. I quickly found myself back in the face of God and returning to the obedience to the Word of God. Many days however, I would sit in my living room reflecting on why I was the only person in my household serving God. Now boredom had slowly turned into loneliness.

It seemed that everyone around me was living their bountiful lives and having the best of times - and taking for granted the grace and mercy of God. They felt that if I was at home praying for everyone, they could do whatever they wanted and could live various lifestyles. I began to get angry with them, because they would always come to me ask me to pray for certain request, instead of them praying for themselves. But they really began dependent on me getting a prayer through on their behalf – Not realizing that I taught them that the effectual fervent prayers of a righteous man avail much.

One thing that can I say for sure is that my family kept me in the face of God. I have cried so many nights on the behalf of myself, my children and my husband. Some situation in life will cause fear to rise; and instead of trusting God and depending on him to work it out – We try to fix it our own way! We feel that either the Lord is moving too slow or he is not moving fast enough. And so, we insert our own plan, only to have to repent and go back to God and trust him to now get us out of the trouble that we have put ourselves in – and then fix the original problem. Now I will admit it is very difficult to "Let Go and Let God" when it's family. Especially when we are the problem solver of the family. But when you realize that he has the Masterplan, and all the answer – Why exhaust yourself and put in all that extra work? I have learned that when I do things my way, without acknowledging him first, I fail every time! But when I put my trust in him and put everything in his hands – He works it out so easily and naturally. Things that I see in the natural eye doesn't look so good, but when I see things with my spiritual eye – He has already worked it out because his promises really are yes and amen!

As a woman of God, I could see all the wrong that my family was doing. I began self-righteous and judgmental. Looking down on them and telling them how horrible of a life they were living and how they needed to be saved. Never encouraging or uplifting – but I thought I was doing the work of the Lord! I did this as though I had or was living a perfect life. I had forgotten all the mistakes that I had made and the several times that I had to repent of my sins. I had to remember that we serve a God of many chance or else he would have left me a long time ago. But Deuteronomy 31:6 promised that he would never leave nor forsake me.

Oftentimes we see others in the way we want them to be instead of seeing them and loving them through the eyes of Christ. Truly I was guilty of this! I wanted my husband and my children to be who I wanted them to be. I honestly believed that if we were all serving God together, that we would have this perfect family. Not realizing that even in salvation there will never be a perfect family! I have realized however, that my family members will have to make the same couscous decision that I had to make – and that is to surrender completely to Jesus Christ for themselves. My pain is what got me to a place of complete surrender to serve him with my whole heart, and the reality is I do not want my family to suffer that kind of pain.

When we begin to consider the lives of others, it's easy to see a perfect family. It can play with your mind. We all want the best spouse in the world, along with the greatest children and grandchildren. So, we see this portrayed by other families it become stuck on repeat – and it plays in your mind repeatedly. Now you began to see all the negative things that your spouse is doing, and you began to see clearly all the mistakes of your children. You began to feel unloved and mistreated, and then loneliness creeps in. Now your children can never seem to get it right and you begin to compare accomplishments with this other family, wondering what is wrong with your family. Why have they not gotten saved yet? Why don't they love me? All of this because you have placed your sight on this perfect family that has rehearsed the lines to their false reality; only to portray it in public, disguising the dreadful reality they share in private.

The enemy really does come to steal, kill and destroy. And he starts with the mind! He will use it as a playground if you allow him to. I will admit it was not easy, but I had to get to a place in Christ to allow my family to live their own lives and to be themselves. I had to come to the realization that I must get to heaven for myself. I will not have the opportunity to stand at the judgment seat with my husband nor my children. Yes, I want them to live a prosperous and holy life! But I have resolved within myself that I have done my due diligence – I have ministered to them and equipped them with the necessary tools to reach God for themselves. And when they are ready to submit to his will, the God that I serve will welcome each of them with open arms.

But even in this revelation, I had to take a good examination of myself. Am I truly walking in the will of God? Am I showing good character and conducting myself in a Christ-like manner at all times? Am I letting my light so shine that men may see his glory and not my own? Do they see an example that they want to emulate? So now I am careful in my walk with Christ. Wherever I go, regardless to who I am around, I must reflect being an ambassador for Christ. I now understand that I cannot change anyone – only God can! And in my marriage, I stand firm to I Corinthians 7:16 that says *the husband is saved through the wife and the same through them both.* We must be careful how we walk this walk with Christ in front of our family, they must see the righteousness of Christ on the inside as well as the outside. I will continue to pray for my family for the rest of my life, and when the day come I will rejoice in the fact that their complete submission will not be through the *salvation in the eyes of me*. But most importantly I have learned to love who stands in front of me – even if they never change.

DAMAGED CHILDREN
HEALING HEARTS TO LOVE AGAIN

TAREN WALTON

CHAPTER EIGHT

FROM PAIN TO PURPOSE

Now get up and stand on your feet. I have appeared to you to appoint you as a servant and as a witness of what you have seen of me and what I will show you. Act 29:16

FROM PAIN TO PURPOSE

Wow! But for the grace of God! Who would of thought that after all that I have been through - the molestation, the rape, the attempted suicide, being promiscuous, the feelings of never being loved and the physical violence. It took all of that for me to realize that my pain was my purpose and that my mess had become the ministry that God had placed on the inside of me. He and only he would get the glory out of my life and his love showed me that my suffering was not in vain. He heard every prayer that I prayed and every tear that I cried. I would have never thought that God would have used such a messy me.

There were days I didn't know what to do or if I would

even live or die. The pain I was in was so severe, but I had to come into the understanding that my tears would be stored in a bottle for someone else to realize my purpose in life which is to help others. When I look back over my life, my soul cries out Hallelujah! It's not a cliché for me – It's my truth. I must give him the praise! God's promises for me are yes and amen. He promised never to leave me. So now I can smile through my tears and the tears that I cry now are tears of joy. I know that my deliverance is in my praise and my worship.

I have developed a relationship with my father who loves me unconditionally and there is no greater love than the love of God. His love is everlasting. Through trial and error, I have learned to love myself. God's love has brought peace to my mind and he restored my joy. I fully understand that I am nothing without him. I am no longer the victim, but through the redemption power of Christ I have become the victor. I will continue to tell my testimony, because I believe that it was only a test. But He knew my destiny. He knew that there would be several times that I would want to give up – throw in the towel; but I will continue to stand on His word. I often remind him of the promises he spoke to me and my family's life. I knew that He had a plan for each one of us - and I know that each one will come to pass.

Gods sees past your hurt and pain and he recognizes that his children have real worth. He is ready to take away the mess that our life has become and offer each of us healing and forgiveness for all the wrong that we have done. It leads us to a whole new way of living where we experience value and we can value others. His love is everlasting!

We must have a prayer life, because when we pray, we

acknowledge God[s presence and it opens a door for Christ to enter in. We must worship Him in spirit and in truth. Our prayers are comforting and encouraging, it eases our very mind and our desires will become more like Him. My prayer is not my will, but His will be done in my life. I had to learn to forgive those that hurt me and mistreated me because I had to realize that forgiveness was not for the ones that hurt me, but forgiveness is intended for me. Forgiveness allows me to be free and no longer be a hostage to anger and resentment.

I had to surrender my all to Him. Therefore, I am learning to fast and pray because Matthew 17:21 tells us that some things are going to come only through fasting and praying. God has done miracles and breakthroughs through my fasting and praying. Oftentimes when things are happening with 0ur families we want to say it's the devil, but sometimes it's Jesus who is exposing some things. We are quick to pray for things seen and unseen and known and unknown. Somethings are hard to accept but we must cast our cares on him. People believe that when you have received his salvation that everything will be OK. There will not be any more pain, but we still go through storms in our lives. We can go through a storm in peace if we trust in him. Isaiah 26:3 tells us that He will keep thee in perfect peace whose mind is stayed on Him. Through our weakness His strength is perfected, we are not perfect, but we strive for perfection daily.

Matthew 22:37 teaches us that Jesus says to love the Lord with all your heart and soul and mind. We as believers have got to show our character and conduct to be Christ-like always. We want our light to shine so that when people see the joy, the peace that we carry, they will want that same love that God has given to us his mercies are new every morning. Philippians 4:13 says we can do all things through Christ Jesus who strengthens us.

Today, as I look at my family I know that God is still working on each and every one of us. My prayer is that my family receive His salvation and that each one will have a relationship with Him. We are all still a work in progress, but just like my mother prayed me through even when I didn't believe, I know my prayers will not fall on a deaf ear, but it shall come to pass. Therefore, all things are possible for them that believe.

When I look at the lives of hurting women and men, God has given me an uncompromising compassion to tell my story. There was a time I kept it to myself because I didn't know how to tell it; because of the embarrassment that I felt. But when God delivered me and set me free I told

Him that I would tell my story everywhere that I go. I don't want to see people suffer the way that I did. I want everyone to know about the goodness of Jesus and all that he has done for me. Because truly, if it had not been for the Lord who was on my side I do not know where I would be today. However, I do know that he saw worth in me; enough worth to use me for His glory. This was all the love that I needed to know to understand that he sees my worth; not only in me – but also in the lives of my children, my husband and my grandchildren. I know there is ministry and purpose on the inside of each of my family members – so no matter what we go through in life or whatever he allows, I have learned to trust his plan. As I continue to pray and trust in Him, I truly thank Him for the great women of God that He has placed in my life, I'm so excited about what He is doing in this season of my life. I am truly grateful for the ministry that He has placed on the inside of me – to help hurting hearts heal and to help others grow both mentally and spiritually.

I am so excited about the new Pen Pal Ministry with Vandalia Women's Prison and Bon'terre Men's Prison. Speaking with these young ladies and visiting with them gives me such a joy. I thank Him every day that I am now walking in my purpose. I give Him all the glory over my life and as I continue my journey in Christ, I will trust in Him on this road From Pain to Purpose.

Made in the USA
Columbia, SC
01 March 2018